Tongue Twisters
Coloring Book

Edited by
Victoria Fremont

Illustrated by
Nina Barbaresi

Dover Publications, Inc.
New York

Published in Canada by General Publishing Company, Ltd., 30 Lesmill Road, Don Mills, Toronto, Ontario.

Published in the United Kingdom by Constable and Company, Ltd., 3 The Lanchesters, 162–164 Fulham Palace Road, London W6 9ER.

Tongue Twisters Coloring Book is a new work, first published by Dover Publications, Inc., in 1993.

International Standard Book Number: 0-486-27736-4

Manufactured in the United States of America
Dover Publications, Inc., 31 East 2nd Street, Mineola, N.Y. 11501

Tongue twisters provide young people with endless hours of enjoyment. They are fun to read aloud and to repeat over and over. Specially selected to appeal to young people today, the 60 tongue twisters in this book are accompanied by delightful illustrations designed to be colored in with pens, pencils or paints. Let your imagination roam as your tongue trips over these tricky phrases! Remember: the short ones need to be repeated several times in order to be challenging.

Peter Piper picked a peck of pickled peppers.
A peck of pickled peppers Peter Piper picked.
If Peter Piper picked a peck of pickled peppers,
Where is the peck of pickled peppers Peter
Piper picked?

Greek grapes.
Greek grapes.
Etc.

Moses supposes his toesies are roses,
But Moses supposes erroneously,
For nobody's toesies are posies of roses,
As Moses supposes his toesies to be.

A big black bug bit a big black bear.

Lemon liniment.
Lemon liniment.
Etc.

Three gray geese in the green grass grazing;
Gray were the geese and green was the grazing.

Thieves seize skis.
Thieves seize skis.
Etc.

Rubber baby buggy bumpers.
Rubber baby buggy bumpers.
Etc.

How much wood would a woodchuck chuck,
  If a woodchuck could chuck wood?
He would chuck, he would, as much as he could,
  If a woodchuck could chuck wood.

Barbara burned the brown bread badly.

Preshrunk shirts.
Preshrunk shirts.
Etc.

11

He ran from the Indies to the Andes in his undies.

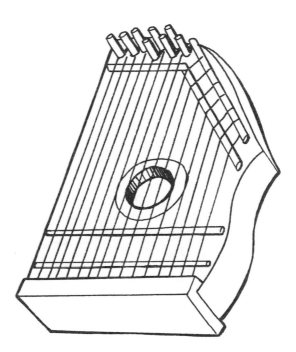

This is a zither. Is this a zither?

I can't stand rotten writing when it's written rotten.

14

Said the flea to the fly as he flew through the
  flue,
"There's a flaw in the floor of the flue."
Said the fly to the flea as he flew through the
  flue,
"A flaw in the floor of the flue doesn't bother me.
Does it bother you?"

15

She sells seashells by the seashore.

A fine field of wheat. A field of fine wheat.

Please, Paul, pause for applause.

Around rough and rugged rocks, the ragged rascal ran.

Don't run along the wrong lane!

This myth is a mystery to me.

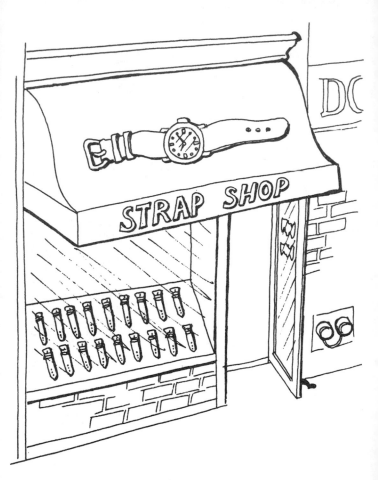

When does the wristwatch-strap shop shut?

Nine nice night nurses nursing nightly.

Double bubble gum bubbles double.

Cheap ship trips.
Cheap ship trips.
Etc.

Tom threw Tim three thumbtacks.

Betty Blue blows big black bubbles.

Wood said he would carry the wood through the wood.

And if Wood said he would, Wood would.

If a dog chews shoes, what shoes should he choose to chew?

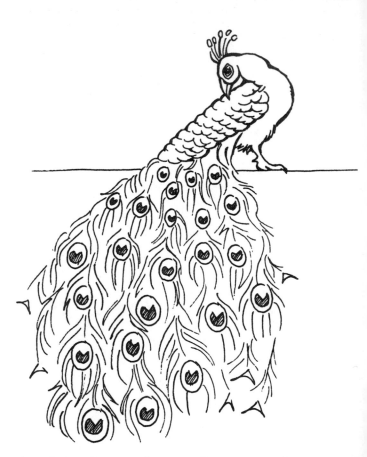

A pale pink proud peacock pompously preened
its pretty plumage.

Of all the felt I ever felt
I never felt a piece of felt
That felt the same as that felt felt,
When I first felt that felt.

A big blue bucket of blue blueberries.

Tom Tire tried to tie his tie twice.

Sip a cup of proper coffee from a proper coffee
   pot.

I never smelled a smelt that smelled as bad as that smelt smelled.

Six southern sailors sailing southern seas.

Greasy Granny grasped the great gray goose.

The sun shines on shop signs.

A tooter who tooted a flute
Tried to tutor two tutors to toot.
  Said the two to the tutor,
  "Is it harder to toot or
To tutor two tutors to toot?"

She says she shall sew a sheet.

Three little ghostesses sitting on postesses,
Eating buttered toastesses,
Greasing their fistesses up to the wristesses,
Oh what beastesses to make such feastesses.

Sure the ship's shipshape, sir.

I saw Esau kissing Kate.
I saw Esau, he saw me.
And she saw I saw Esau.

Yellow yo-yos.
Yellow yo-yos.
44   Etc.

A skunk sat on a stump.
The skunk thunk the stump stunk,
And the stump thunk the skunk stunk.

Betty beat a bit of butter to make a better batter.

Who washed Washington's white woolen under-
wear when Washington's washerwoman went
West?

Twelve tall tulips turning to the sun.

Naughty Nettie's knitting knotted nighties for the Navy.

The swan swims!
The swan swam!
The swimming swan swam on the sea!

A box of biscuits, a box of mixed biscuits, and a
biscuit mixer.

Does this shop stock short socks with spots?

Sister Susie's sewing shirts for soldiers.

I thought a thought.

But the thought I thought wasn't the thought
I thought I thought.

If the thought I thought I thought had been
the thought I thought, I wouldn't have thought
so much.

54

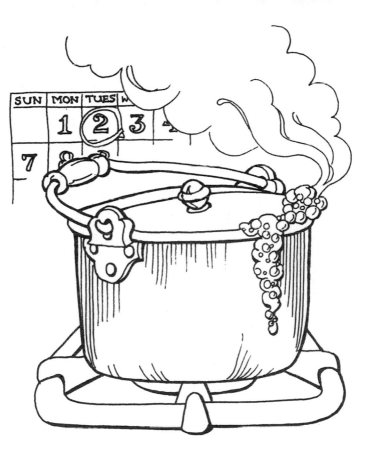

Tuesday is stew day.
Stew day is Tuesday.

Pop and popped popcorn.
Pop and popped popcorn.

Etc.

Over the river . . . a lump of raw liver.

Toy boat.
Toy boat.
Etc.

Sheep shouldn't sleep in a shack.
Sheep should sleep in a shed.

If two witches were watching two watches,
which witch would watch which watch?